Vatican II: *Act II*

An Adult Discussion Program

Robert L. Kinast

CALLED TO HOLINESS

Participant's Guide

A Program of The National Pastoral Life Center

A Liturgical Press Book

While the authors and editors of *Vatican II: Act II* are sensitive to the use of inclusive language, they did not deem it proper to alter the wording of the documents of Vatican II and Scripture used in this book.

Fr. Robert L. Kinast, director of the Center for Theological Reflection, Madeira Beach, Florida, is the principal author of this discussion program.

Cover design by Don Bruno

Nihil obstat: Joseph C. Kremer, Th.D. *Censor Deputatus.*
Imprimatur: ✠ Jerome Hanus, O.S.B., Bishop of St. Cloud, June 12, 1992.

ISBN 0-8146-2143-0

Contents

Foreword

"It is in relation to Vatican II that modern Catholics live their faith, whether they realize it or not. Vatican II is the point of reference for the modern Catholic Church." How significant this quotation from *Vatican II: Act II*. The Second Vatican Council has truly become part of the air we breathe.

A significant aspect of that change of climate brought on by Vatican II is the communal nature of the Church. Perhaps in no way has the Second Vatican Council become a more meaningful point of reference for Catholics than in the way parishioners today experience community in the Sunday Eucharist, in the other sacramental celebrations, and in the growing number of small faith sharing communities that have sprung up around the world.

Small communities alone enjoy a remarkably different role and acceptance in the scheme of parish life today as compared to thirty years ago. Once engaged in by "Catholic Action types" at the periphery of the parish, they now involve a healthy percentage of parishioners in the mainstream of parish life.

So accepted has the value of small communities come to be that in *Small Christian Communities: A Vision of Hope* those of us who have worked with RENEW recently identified three types of small groups and communities for which we offer practical organizing advice. *Seasonal small groups* foster the spiritual growth of large numbers of parishioners; *ministerial communities* offer a strong base for all ministry; and *small Christian communities* call for a deep commitment to a holistic spirituality that seeks to transform all of life and society.

The support for small communities in parishes truly calls for a great amount of care and nurturing. On several counts *Vatican II: Act II* fits the bill well. Designed specifically for use by popular seasonal groups, it enables them to move past reflections that tend to linger on personal piety. Parishioners will be challenged to move beyond the level of personal comfort in their seasonal group to respond to Vatican II's call to responsible involvement and evangelization. *Vatican II: Act II* will do the same for ministerial communities as they see their call in faith to embrace substantially more than the ministry of their choosing. For small Christian communities it will provide the substance for study that enables enlightened decisions and sound actions for connecting the gospel and the marketplace.

In all of this *Vatican II: Act II* gives us a wealth of much needed material that provides for solid small group and small community growth. What finer source of ideas and formation than the very teachings and guidance of the Church in council? What surer way to know that directions taken are inspired by the Holy Spirit? Small Christian communities offer great hope for the future. They contribute to a vision that gives us an ideal to move toward as we enter the third millennium. *Vatican II: Act II* takes a fine stride in the right direction of enabling that vision to walk.

Rev. Msgr. Thomas A. Kleissler
Founder and Director of RENEW

Introduction

VATICAN II

Vatican II was a series of meetings of all the Roman Catholic bishops of the world, convened by the Pope. Such meetings are called ''general'' or ''ecumenical'' (worldwide) councils. Prior to Vatican II there had been only twenty such councils in the history of the Church.

Vatican II lasted from 1962 to 1965. The meetings themselves were held in the fall, usually beginning in October and ending in December. The council was called by Pope John XXIII, who died after the first session, and was concluded by Pope Paul VI.

The overall purpose of the council was to examine the Church in order to renew its internal life, support the movement for Christian unity (ecumenism), and contribute to the solution of problems in the modern world.

The most tangible result was the sixteen documents the council produced. These consist of four constitutions, which discuss theological issues; nine decrees, which present principles for Church action; and three declarations, which discuss issues outside the Church.

The council documents set forth the vision and direction of the Church. This is not a single, uniform vision but a combination of viewpoints, of many sources of spiritual energy that seek constantly to work together. Subsequent documents and developments find their basis in these documents of Vatican II.

The official name of each document is taken from the first words in its Latin text. The documents, together with their English titles and main themes, are listed at the back of this book.

The council has had a far-reaching impact, described here under four headings:

Postconciliar documents. Numerous documents have been produced since the council to implement, clarify, or develop the principles set down by Vatican II, especially those regarding liturgy and ecumenism. A sampling of the postconciliar documents is found in the two volumes *Vatican Council II: The Conciliar and Post Conciliar Documents* and *Vatican Council II: More Post Conciliar Documents,* published by The Liturgical Press, Collegeville, Minnesota. In addition, this program quotes from the apostolic exhortation of Pope John Paul II entitled *The Vocation and Mission of the Lay Faithful in the Church and in the World,* which was issued following the 1987 Synod on the Laity.

Structures. In order to implement the vision of Vatican II, new structures have been developed. These include national conferences of bishops, priests' councils, and diocesan and parish pastoral councils. To continue worldwide consultation between the Pope and the bishops, synods of bishops are held approximately every three years, with a representative number of bishops from every country attending.

Priorities. Today, spirituality is fostered through liturgy more than through personal devotions, and within the liturgy emphasis is on participation rather than on mere attendance. Scripture is more central than catechism; an ecumenical spirit of openness and cooperation is evident in relations with other Christians; the laity are seen as equal partners with clergy and religious in the ministry of the Church; concern for the poor of our society is cultivated through action for social change rather than through charity alone.

Experiences. Closely aligned with new priorities are new experiences of being Catholic. Among these is the experience of community, often nurtured in small groups that have a prayer-sharing focus. In like manner, the experience of liturgy, of the clergy, of adult faith, of other Christians and other religions, of social commitment, have all been affected by Vatican II. It is in relation to Vatican II that modern Catholics live their faith, whether they realize it or not. Vatican II is the point of reference for the modern Catholic Church.

VATICAN II—ACT II

Vatican II—Act II provides a format for studying the Vatican II documents, reflecting on the impact they continue to have, and responding to the Church's challenge to action. The six-session program is for adults who are serious about living as Catholics in today's world under the influence of Vatican II. It is designed to keep the vision of Vatican II alive by recalling its message and relating it to contemporary experience.

The present topic, *Called to Holiness,* looks at the theme of spirituality as lived out in everyday circumstances and families, using the Bible and liturgy to respond to God's call to holiness. We examine what Vatican II said as well as our response to the council's message. Important to the program is the concept that learning must lead to action; both learning and action are stressed throughout. An optional seventh session is included, designed for planning and carrying out an action based on the group's understanding of Vatican II principles.

After completing *Called to Holiness,* groups could decide to begin another six-session program, such as *Living in God's World* or *Families.*

Vatican II—Act II is meant to be used by small groups meeting in the parish or in the homes of members. Each session is designed for an hour-and-a-half time period, plus about a half-hour preparation time for the session. Each participant should have a copy of the *Participant's Guide.* The group leader should have a copy of the *Convener's Guide* and should be prepared to lead the discussions.

SESSION ONE

Holiness: Who Is Called?

Goals

- To share personal descriptions of holy people
- To learn what Vatican II said about the call to holiness
- To put this learning into practice through action

Scripture

Imagine that St. Paul is writing to you personally. As you hear his exhortation, think of times when you have done what he asks and times when you have not.

Colossians 3:12-16 **Because you are God's chosen ones, holy and beloved, clothe yourselves with heartfelt mercy, with kindness, humility, meekness; forgive whatever grievances you have against one another. Forgive as the Lord has forgiven you. Over all these virtues put on love, which binds the rest together and makes them perfect. Christ's peace must reign in your hearts, since as members of one body you have been called to that peace. Dedicate yourselves to thankfulness. Let the word of Christ, rich as it is, dwell in you. In wisdom made perfect, instruct and admonish one another. Sing gratefully to God from your hearts in psalms, hymns, and inspired songs.**

Prayer

O Holy God, you call each of us to become like you. You do not ask us to cease being human in order to become holy but to cultivate our feelings, thoughts, relationships, and experiences in harmony with you. In our time together help us to do this with one another. We ask this through Christ our Lord. Amen.

Who Is Holy?

Take a few minutes to complete the following statements.

The holiest person I have ever known or known about is

____

The thing I admire most about this person is

____

____

____

Comments from others in the group:

____

____

____

____

How many of the "holiest people" listed by the group are well known (i.e., canonized saints, public figures) and how many are not well known? What does this say about the group's understanding of holiness?

Does one need to possess all the qualities listed to be holy? What does this say about the group's understanding of holiness?

Vatican II Speaks

The renewal of the spiritual life was one of the primary goals of Vatican II. The council spoke directly about holiness and spirituality in the Dogmatic Constitution on the Church, chapter 5. It made three important points.

1. The call to Christian holiness is centered on Christ. "The Lord Jesus, divine teacher and model of all perfection, preached holiness of life (of which he is the author and maker) to each and every one of his disciples without distinction: 'You, therefore, must be perfect, as your heavenly Father is perfect' " (no. 40).
2. Everyone is called to a holy life. "It is therefore quite clear that all Christians in any state or walk of life are called to the fullness of Christian life and to the perfection of love, and by this holiness a more human manner of life is fostered also in earthly society" (no. 40).
3. Everyone becomes holy in and through the particular circumstances of their lives, for example, raising children, working, making decisions, fulfilling responsibilities, participating in social and political activity. "The forms and tasks of life are many but holiness is one—that sanctity which is cultivated by all who act under God's Spirit and, obeying the Father's voice and adoring God the Father in spirit and truth, follow Christ, poor, humble and cross-bearing, that they may deserve to be partakers of his glory. Each one, however, according to their own gifts and duties must steadfastly advance along

the way of a living faith, which arouses hope and works through love'' (no. 41).

We can't discuss every circumstance or experience through which people become holy, so for the next four sessions we will focus on those the council highlighted:

everyday spirituality
family spirituality
biblical spirituality
liturgical spirituality

We hope to enrich each other through these discussions, to learn what Vatican II had to say, and to put what we learn into practice.

Summing Up

One of the major goals of Vatican II was the spiritual renewal of each member of the Church. The council stressed that all persons are called to holiness in Christ and they respond to this call in the ordinary circumstances of their lives.

To sharpen what you've learned from the first session, answer the following:

Before this discussion, I thought holiness meant

Praying more than anyone else
Not being very human

Now I think holiness means

Doing God's will in all aspects of life.
To have the desire to be with God

Action

To personalize my understanding of holiness, I can arrange to meet someone whom I regard to be holy and to discuss with that person what enables him or her to be that way.

To deepen my experience of holiness, I can spend five minutes a day reading a favorite gospel story and think about how it applies to my life.

To acquaint myself with resources for holiness, I can find out what spiritual opportunities are being offered in my parish or diocese and take advantage of them.

Before the Next Session

Carry out one of the Action suggestions.

Complete your answers to the Summing Up questions if you did not have a chance to do so during the session itself. Reread your answers before the next session.

Read the Home Study Questions for this session, and read the Home Study Questions for Session 2, pages 22–24; or read Chapter 5, Dogmatic Constitution on the Church.

Closing Prayer

O God, you call us to holiness in the very web of our existence, in and through the events of daily life, the complex decisions and conflicting values we struggle with, the richness and fragility of our sexual relationships, to maintain a delicate balance between activity and stillness, presence and privacy, love and loss. Through it all, help us to find you in Christ Jesus our Lord. Amen.

—Based on *Called and Gifted,* the U.S. bishops' reflections on the laity

Home Study Questions

Is there a difference between holiness and spirituality?

Vatican II did not make a sharp distinction between holiness and spirituality. In general, the council used the term "holiness" to refer to the state or condition of being in union with God or Christ. This is also called the state of perfection or sanctity. It used the term "spirituality" or the spiritual life to refer to those activities and resources that deepen and express the state of holiness. In this sense, you might think of holiness as the goal and spirituality as the means.

In the Dogmatic Constitution on the Church the council expressed this as follows:

> In order to reach this perfection [holiness] the faithful should use the strength dealt out to them by Christ's gift, so that, following in his footsteps and conformed to his image, doing the will of God in everything, they may wholeheartedly devote themselves to the glory of God and to the service of their neighbor. Thus the holiness of the People of God will grow in fruitful abundance, as is clearly shown in the history of the Church through the life of so many saints (no. 40).

In the Decree on the Apostolate of Lay People the council made the same point under the heading "The Spirituality of Lay People."

> This life of intimate union with Christ in the Church is maintained by the spiritual helps common to all the faithful, chiefly by active participation in the liturgy. Laymen should make such a use of these helps that, while meeting their human obligations in the ordinary conditions of life, they do not separate their union with Christ from their ordinary life; but through the very performance of their tasks, which are God's will for them, actually promote the growth of their union with him (no. 4).

Even if everyone is called to holiness, don't some people receive a higher call than others?

Vatican II tried to avoid ranking the different vocations in the Church. It preferred to stress the contribution of each to the whole Church and to point out the ways they complement one another. For example, in the Dogmatic Constitution on the Church, the council said, "Everything that has been said of the People of God is addressed equally to laity, religious, and clergy" (no. 30).

Similarly, in the Decree on the Church's Missionary Activity, Vatican II declared:

> The Church is not truly established and does not fully live, nor is a perfect sign of Christ unless there is a genuine laity existing and working alongside the hierarchy. For the Gospel cannot become deeply rooted in the mentality, life and work of a people without the active presence of lay people (no. 21).

This equal and complementary role in ministry is true of spirituality also. Pope John Paul II made this clear.

> Everyone in the Church, precisely because they are members, receive and thereby share in the common vocation to holiness. In the fullness of this title and on equal par with all other members of the Church, the lay faithful are called to holiness (Apostolic Exhortation on the Christian Lay Faithful, no. 16).

What about religious orders? What does it mean to follow "the evangelical counsels"?

Vatican II generally avoided language that would give the impression that some people are more perfect than others just because they belong to a particular group or way of life.

Regarding religious orders, Vatican II stressed that each of them is a different expression of the Church's common holiness and contributes to the richness of the Church as a whole:

> . . . a wonderful variety of religious communities came into existence. This has considerably contributed towards enabling the Church not merely to be equipped for every good work and to be prepared for the work of the ministry unto the building-up of the Body of Christ, but also to appear adorned with the manifold gifts

> of her children, like a bride adorned for her husband, and to manifest in herself the multiform wisdom of God (Decree on the Up-to-Date Renewal of Religious Life, no. 1).

Members of religious orders ordinarily make a public profession of three vows, which are considered a special form of union with Christ. The vows are poverty, chastity, and obedience. They are called evangelical counsels because they take their origin from the gospel accounts of Jesus' life.

How far does this diversity in the spiritual life extend?

Vatican II took a wide, inclusive view of the spiritual life. It acknowledged diversity within the Catholic Church, not only through members of religious orders but also through those in the various cultures throughout the world.

> They must give expression to this newness of life in their own society and culture and in a manner that is in keeping with the traditions of their own land. They must be familiar with this culture, they must purify and guard it, they must develop it in accordance with present-day conditions, they must perfect it in Christ so that the faith of Christ and the life of the Church will not be something foreign to the society in which they live, but will begin to transform and permeate it (Decree on the Church's Missionary Activity, no 21).

Another example of spiritual diversity within the Roman Catholic Church is the respect shown to the various Eastern Rites.

> History, tradition and very many ecclesiastical institutions give clear evidence of the great debt owed to the Eastern Church by the Church Universal. Therefore the holy council not merely praises and appreciates as is due this ecclesiastical and spiritual heritage, but also insists on viewing it as the heritage of the whole Church of Christ (Decree on the Catholic Eastern Churches, no. 5).

Regarding Orthodox Christians, the council said:

> From their very origins the Churches of the East have had a treasury from which the Church of the West has drawn largely for its liturgy, spiritual tradition, and jurisprudence (Decree on Ecumenism, no. 14).

Regarding other Christians, the council said:

> Some, even very many, of the most significant elements and endowments which together go to build up and give life to the Church itself, can exist outside the visible boundaries of the Catholic Church: the written Word of God; the life of grace; faith, hope and charity, with the other interior gifts of the Holy Spirit, as well as visible elements (no. 3).

In addition, the council called for a "spiritual ecumenism" as the soul of the whole ecumenical movement (no. 8).

Regarding Jews, the council said:

> Sounding the depths of the mystery which is the Church, this sacred Council remembers the spiritual ties which link the people of the New Covenant to the stock of Abraham (Declaration on the Relation of the Church to Non-Christian Religions, no. 4).

The council went on to say:

> Since Christians and Jews have such a common spiritual heritage, this sacred Council wishes to encourage and further mutual understanding and appreciation. This can be obtained, especially, by way of biblical and theological enquiry and through friendly discussions (no. 4).

Regarding other religions the council said:

> In Hinduism men explore the divine mystery and express it both in the limitless riches of myth and the accurately defined insights of philosophy. They seek release from the trials of the present life by ascetical practices, profound meditation, and recourse to God in confidence and love (no. 2).
>
> Buddhism in its various forms testifies to the essential inadequacy of this changing world. It proposes a way of life by which men can, with confidence and trust, attain a state of perfect liberation and reach supreme illumination either through their own efforts or by the aid of divine help (no. 2).
>
> Muslims . . . worship God, who is one, living and subsistent, merciful and almighty, the Creator of heaven and earth, who has also spoken to men. They strive to submit themselves without reserve to the hidden decrees of God, just as Abraham submitted himself to God's plan, to whose faith Muslims eagerly link their own (no. 3).

Regarding contemporary people in general, Vatican II said:

> This demand for freedom in human society is concerned chiefly with man's spiritual values, and especially with what concerns the free practice of religion in society. This Vatican Council pays careful attention to these spiritual aspirations (Declaration on Religious Liberty, no. 1).

If everyone is called to holiness, what does the Church do to help people respond to this call?

Vatican II customarily spoke of this help as ''formation'' in the spiritual life. In its documents the council addressed the formation of different groups, not offering many specifics but listing principles that would govern the spiritual life.

Regarding religious orders, Vatican II listed these principles as *(a)* the following of Christ as it is put before us in the Gospel; *(b)* the spirit and aims of the community's founder; *(c)* sharing in the biblical, liturgical, dogmatic, pastoral, ecumenical, missionary, and social life of the Church; *(d)* a proper understanding of the human person, of the conditions of the times, and of the needs of the Church; and *(e)* the priority of spiritual renewal (Decree on the Up-to-Date Renewal of Religious Life, no. 2).

Regarding candidates for the priesthood, Vatican II said:

> Spiritual formation should be closely associated with doctrinal and pastoral formation, and, with the assistance of the spiritual director in particular, should be conducted in such a way that the students may learn to live in intimate and unceasing union with God the Father through his Son Jesus Christ, in the Holy Spirit. Those who are to take on the likeness of Christ the priest by sacred ordination should form the habit of drawing close to him as friends in every detail of their lives (Decree on the Training of Priests, no. 8).

Regarding laypersons, Vatican II stressed the same "life of intimate union with Christ in the Church" and recommended the following spiritual helps: active participation in the liturgy; performance of their tasks in life; and exercising the virtue of faith with meditation on Scripture, of hope with meditation on the cross and resurrection, and of love with meditation on the Beatitudes (Decree on the Apostolate of Lay People, no. 4).

Pope John Paul II reaffirmed this view when he said: "There is no doubt that spiritual formation ought to occupy a privileged place in a person's life." He then drew attention to the value of doctrinal formation, a Christian promotion of culture, awareness of the Church's social doctrine, and cultivation of human values (Apostolic Exhortation on the Christian Lay Faithful, no. 60).

The Pope also stressed that the parish "has the essential task of a more personal and immediate formation of the lay faithful." Within the parish, "small Church communities, where present, can be a notable help in the formation of Christians, by providing a consciousness and an experience of ecclesial communion and mission which are more extensive and incisive" than the parish as a whole can provide (no. 61).

No matter what the forms and resources, however, the ultimate key to formation in Christian spirituality is "the help that diverse members of the Church can give to each other" (no. 61).

SESSION TWO

Everyday Spirituality: What Counts?

Goals

- To consider the spiritual challenges and opportunities of people in diverse circumstances
- To learn how Vatican II stressed daily activity as a source of spirituality
- To put this learning into practice through action

Scripture

This Scripture passage is the conclusion of the section from St. Paul we heard last time. As you remember, Paul listed the qualities of Christian holiness. Recall the quality you prayed for in your own life. Now listen as Paul says:

Colossians 3:17 **Whatever you do, whether in speech or in action, do it in the name of the Lord Jesus. Give thanks to God the Father through him.**

Prayer

O Loving God, you set before us a wonderful scene, countless people busy at work in their daily lives, perhaps far from public view and unacclaimed by others but cherished by you, for these are the humble yet great builders of your kingdom. Count us among them in union with Christ our Lord. Amen.

—Based on Pope John Paul II's Exhortation on the Christian Lay Faithful, no. 17

Three Journals

St. Paul encourages us to do everything in the name of the Lord Jesus. But often there are so many things to do that we lose sight of the spiritual significance of ordinary activities. Sometimes we might think that people with other vocations have it easier.

Journal 1: It's getting harder and harder to find just ten minutes a day for personal prayer. Some days I have to rely on my ten-minute walk from the office to the parking lot. During those walks I pick out one event and think about what God was asking me in that situation. (Parish staff)

Journal 2: The pace never stopped today. If it wasn't the phone, it was some other interruption. God knows, I'm sure, how hectic it gets juggling the demands of family, work, neighbors, and church. I've heard people say that their activity is their prayer. That sounds appealing but I'm not sure what it means. (Business person)

Journal 3: I visited my neighbor, Louise, at the cancer center today. We've known each other a long time but we've never talked as personally as we have since her cancer was diagnosed. She has accepted her condition with such faith and God seems so real to her that it is truly a spiritual experience for me to be with her.

Which of the journals best describes your own experience?

______Journal 1 __✓__Journal 2 ______Journal 3

Looking at that journal, would you say the daily activity of the person is a help or a hindrance to their spirituality?

______Help __✓__Hindrance

If a hindrance, what advice would you give to make it a help?

Always begin the day dedicating everything to the greater glory of God. Try during the day to briefly rededicate all actions to the greater glory of God. Motivation of action is the key

If a help, how is it applicable in your life?

____

____

____

Who do you think wrote each of the journals?

Journal 1 ________________________________

Journal 2 ________________________________

Journal 3 ________________________________

Vatican II Speaks

For a long time many people in the Church thought that only those in religious orders or those ordained to the priesthood were truly holy. To be holy you had to leave the ordinary activities of life. As we saw in the last session, Vatican II tried to change this impression.

''All the faithful are invited and obliged to holiness and the perfection of their own state of life'' (Dogmatic Constitution on the Church, no. 42).

The council spelled this out by describing the primary activities of various ''states of life.''

PARENTS

''Christian married couples and parents, following their own way, should support one another in grace all through life with faithful love, and should train their children (lovingly received from God) in Christian doctrine and evangelical virtues'' (no. 41).

LABORERS

''Those who engage in human work, often of a heavy kind, should perfect themselves through it, help their fellow-citizens, and promote the betterment of the whole of human society and the whole of creation'' (no. 41).

MINISTERS

The bishop provides the model for all ministers who ''should carry out their ministry with holiness and eagerness, with humility and fortitude; thus fulfilled, this ministry will also be for them an outstanding means of sanctification'' (no. 41).

SUFFERERS

''In a special way also, those who are weighed down by poverty, infirmity, sickness and other hardships should realize that they are united to Christ, who suffers for the salvation of the world; let those feel the same who suffer persecution for the sake of justice'' (no. 41).

How do these descriptions relate to the three journals? to your own life?

UNITED TO CHRIST

Vatican II did not have specific answers for each person's situation, but it did encourage everyone to see their own daily activity as a way of deepening their union with Jesus the Priest, Prophet, and Pastor.

Union with Christ the Priest:

> For all their works, prayers and apostolic undertakings, family and married life, daily work, relaxation of mind and body, if they are accomplished in the Spirit—indeed even the hardships of life if patiently borne—all these become spiritual sacrifices acceptable to God through Jesus Christ (no. 34).

Union with Christ the Prophet:

> Evangelization, that is, the proclamation of Christ by word and the testimony of life, acquires a specific property and peculiar efficacy because it is accomplished in the ordinary circumstances of the world (no. 35).

Union with Christ the Pastor:

> Even by their secular activity they [the laity] must aid one another to greater holiness of life so that the world may be filled with the spirit of Christ and may the more effectively attain its destiny in justice, in love, and in peace (no. 36).

Summing Up

Vatican II affirmed that God calls each person to holiness through the circumstances of daily life. Whatever these circumstances may be, they can lead to a deeper union with Christ the Priest, Prophet, and Pastor.

One daily activity of mine that could be an aid to my spirituality is

Cooking

One way I can make this activity part of my spiritual life is

To do it with love and do it well so that it is good + nourishing for the family

Action

To develop my everyday spirituality, I can keep a journal of my daily activities and reflect on their spiritual significance by myself or with others.

To stimulate my everyday spirituality, I can concentrate on one spiritual value (patience, generosity, encouragement of others) and look for daily opportunities to practice it.

To challenge my everyday spirituality, I can join (or form) a group of parishioners to meet the needs of the poor, the lonely, the suffering.

Before the Next Session

Carry out one of the Action suggestions.

Read the Home Study Questions for Session 3, pages 29–31; or read Chapter 1, Decree on the Apostolate of Lay People.

Complete the questionnaire for the next session on pages 25–26.

Closing Prayer

O God, you have called each of us by name to live your own communion of love and holiness and to be one in the great family of your children. Help us in our daily activity to shine with the light of Christ and to communicate the fire of the Spirit in every part of society through our life inspired by the Gospel. We ask this through Christ our Lord. Amen.

—Based on the prayer of John Paul II, Exhortation on the Christian Lay Faithful

Home Study Questions

Don't you have to pray to make everyday activities holy? Isn't that just adding one more activity?

Prayer *is* essential, but Vatican II's understanding of prayer was not so much "saying prayers" as living a real, sacramental union with Christ in everything you do. The goal is for Christians to live a single spiritual life that encompasses everything rather than living two lives: "While meeting their human obligations in the ordinary conditions of life, they do not separate their union with Christ from their ordinary life" (Decree on the Lay Apostolate, no. 4).

Pope John Paul II put it this way:

> There cannot be two parallel lives in their existence: on the one hand, the so-called "spiritual" life, with its values and demands; and on the other, the so-called "secular" life, that is life in a family, at work, in social relationships, in the responsibilities of public life, and in culture (Apostolic Exhortation on the Christian Lay Faithful, no. 59).

This sounds like an activist spirituality. What happened to meditation, spiritual reading, silence, private devotions?

Vatican II certainly affirmed these traditional spiritual exercises, but in doing so, it remained true to its own principle that "all Christians, in the conditions, duties, and circumstances of their life and through all these, will sanctify themselves more and more if they receive all things with faith from the hand of the heavenly Father and cooperate with the divine will, thus showing forth in that temporal service the love with which God has loved the world" (Dogmatic Constitution on the Church, no. 41).

Most people are very active, and that formed the focus of the council's comments on spirituality. When it did talk about praying throughout the day, Vatican II stressed the Liturgy of the Hours, which is also known as the Divine Office.

What is the Liturgy of the Hours?

As Vatican II explained in The Constitution on the Sacred Liturgy, "the divine office, in keeping with ancient Christian tradition, is so devised that the whole course of the day and night is made holy by the praise of God" (no. 84). This is done by praying assigned psalms and singing hymns at various times during the day.

Ordinarily the full office is prayed by those in monastic orders, while members of apostolic religious communities, diocesan priests, and laity pray Morning and Evening Prayer and any other parts they can, taking account of "the conditions of modern life in which those who are engaged in apostolic work must live" (no. 89).

What about the laity? The Liturgy of the Hours isn't really for them, is it?

The council encouraged participation of the laity in all forms of the liturgy, including the Liturgy of the Hours. In this respect Vatican II said:

> Pastors of souls should see to it that the principle hours, especially Vespers [Evening Prayer], are celebrated in common in church on Sundays and on the more solemn feasts. The laity, too, are encouraged to recite the divine office, either with the priests, or among themselves, or even individually (The Constitution on the Sacred Liturgy, no. 100).

Obviously, for most people this is not the most convenient way to bring everyday activity into harmony with the spiritual life. But priests and religious who do active ministry face the same challenge. The council's advice to them is applicable to all Christians.

Regarding the religious, Vatican II drew a connection between their service and the cultivation of virtues in the spiritual life:

> This service of God should stimulate and foster the exercise of the virtues by them, especially the virtues of humility and obedience, fortitude and chastity, by which they share in Christ's emptying of himself and at the same time in his life in the spirit (Decree on the Up-to-Date Renewal of Religious Life, no. 5).

Regarding priests, Vatican II said the same thing, with a clear emphasis on baptism:

> Like all Christians they have already received in the consecration of baptism the sign and gift of their great calling and grace. . . . In this way they are made strong in the life of the spirit by exercising the ministration of the Spirit and of justice. . . . For it is through the sacred actions they perform every day, as through their whole

> ministry which they exercise in union with the bishop and their fellow-priests, that they are set on the right course to perfection of life (Decree on the Ministry and Life of Priests, no. 12).

Regarding the laity, Vatican II said:

> On life's pilgrimage they are hidden with Christ in God, are free from the slavery of riches, are in search of the goods that last for ever. Generously they exert all their energies in extending God's kingdom, in making the Christian spirit a vital energizing force in the temporal sphere. In life's trials they draw courage from hope, "convinced that present sufferings are no measure of the future glory to be revealed in us" (Decree on the Apostolate of Lay People, no. 4).

Pope John Paul II has expressed the same sentiment, implying that the key to everyday spirituality is not more activity but doing one's daily tasks in the spirit of Christ as an extension of one's baptismal union.

> The eyes of faith behold a wonderful scene: that of a countless number of lay people, both women and men, busy at work in their daily life and activity, oftentimes far from view and quite unacclaimed by the world, unknown to the world's great personages but nonetheless looked upon in love by the Father, untiring laborers who work in the Lord's vineyard. Confident and steadfast through the power of God's grace, these are the humble yet great builders of the Kingdom of God in history (Exhortation on the Christian Lay Faithful, no. 17).

SESSION THREE

Family Spirituality: How Close to Home?

Goals

- To identify family experiences that aid the spiritual life
- To learn what Vatican II said about family spirituality
- To see the spiritual benefits of extended families as well as relations between families
- To put this learning into practice through action

Scripture

One of Jesus' most dramatic cures is narrated in Luke 8:26-39. After Jesus freed a man who was possessed, the spirits entered a nearby herd of swine and drove them over the cliff.

Luke 8:38-39 **The man from whom the spirits had departed asked to come with him, but Jesus sent him away with the words, "Go back home and recount all that God has done for you." The man went all through the town making public what Jesus had done for him.**

Prayer

O God, keep us in love with each other so that the peace of Christ may stay with us and always be in our homes. May our families strengthen us so we may bear witness to your love in this world. We ask this through Christ our Lord. Amen.

—Based on the blessing at the end of the rite of marriage

Family Experiences

Most people are part of several families (for example, family of origin, extended family, one's own family, family of friends). Each family has its own experiences and activities. Some of them help our spiritual growth, some of them don't. Look at the following lists and check the items that apply to you. Feel free to add other experiences.

In my experience of family, what has brought me closest to God is:

___✓___the birth of a child
_______relations with siblings
___✓___becoming a grandparent
___✓___vacations
___✓___facing a family crisis
___✓___making love with my spouse
___✓___helping families in need

____

____

In my experience of family, what has kept me from growing spiritually is:

______obligations to the children
______money worries
______work
______facing a family crisis
______in-laws
______pressure to get married

____

____

Notes from the group

____

____

____

____

Vatican II Speaks

> Married partners have their own proper vocation: they must be witnesses of faith and love of Christ to one another and to their children. The Christian family proclaims aloud both the present power of the kingdom of God and the hope of the blessed life. Hence, by example and by their testimony, they convict the world of sin and give light to those who seek the truth (Dogmatic Constitution on the Church, no. 35).

When Vatican II spoke of families, it said in effect that by doing what they are supposed to do, spouses and parents grow spiritually. This has its effect on children, just as children have their effect on parents.

> Inspired by the example and family prayer of their parents, children, and in fact everyone living under the family roof, will more easily set out upon the path of a truly human training, of salvation, and of holiness. . . . Children as living members of the family contribute in their own way to the sanctification of their parents (Pastoral Constitution on the Church in the Modern World, no. 48)

How do these passages compare to your list of family experiences?

How do children contribute to the spirituality of family?

How do friends of the family aid family spirituality?

LIFE BETWEEN FAMILIES

In addition to the experiences within a family, there are important spiritual experiences between families. Vatican II described this importance as follows:

> The Christian family springs from marriage, which is an image and a sharing in the partnership of love between Christ and the Church; it will show forth to all Christ's living presence in the world and the authentic nature of the Church by the love and generous fruitfulness of the spouses, by their unity and fidelity, and by the loving way in which all members of the family cooperate with each other (Pastoral Constitution on the Church in the Modern World, no. 48).

Regarding specific works of the family, described as "the family apostolate," Vatican II cited

> adopting abandoned children, showing a loving welcome to strangers, helping with the running of schools, supporting adolescents with advice and help, assisting engaged couples to make a better preparation for marriage, taking a share in catechism, teaching, supporting married people and families in material and moral crisis, and in the case of the aged not only providing them with what is indispensable but also procuring for them a fair share of the fruits of economic progress (Decree on the Apostolate of Lay People, no. 11).

These activities are not considered "busy work" or something to do when not praying. They are the very means of family spirituality.

"Christian couples are, for each other, for their children and for their relatives, cooperators of grace and witnesses of the faith" (no. 11).

How does this connection between family activities and spirituality strike you? What other activities would you list?

EXTENDED FAMILIES

There is always a tendency when speaking of family to think only of the nuclear family of parents and children living in one dwelling. Vatican II acknowledged other family situations when it said, "in a different way, a similar example is given by widows and single people who can also greatly contribute to the holiness and activity of the church" (Dogmatic Constitution on the Church, no. 41).

The council did not spell out these contributions nor did it say more about the particular spirituality of people in these circumstances. But it did recall this general point when it spoke of lay spirituality as taking "its particular character from the circumstances of one's state in life (married and family, celibacy, widowhood), from one's state of health, and from one's professional and social activity" (Decree on the Apostolate of Lay People, no. 4).

From your experience, what more could be said about the spirituality of the extended family?

______

______

______

of families which experience divorce or some other disruption?

______

______

______

of groups or communities whose relationships are described as a "family"?

______

______

______

Summing Up

Vatican II saw family life as a primary source of spirituality. This includes the life within a family, within an extended family, and between families of all types. Both the joys and sorrows, the successes and challenges, of family life can nourish spirituality.

In light of the discussion, I would say the three most important things about family spirituality are

1. ______

______

2. ______

______

3. ______

______

Action

If I live in a family with children, I could suggest we take turns leading a family meal prayer or night prayer.

If I live in a family with older children or teenagers, I could invite their friends to one of our family events.

To extend my family spirituality, I could find out what my parish is doing for widowed, divorced, or single parents and consider how I or my family can help.

Before the Next Session

Carry out one of the Action suggestions.

Complete the statements on page 33.

Read the Home Study Questions for Session 4, pages 36–38; or read Part II, Chapter 1, Pastoral Constitution on the Church in the Modern World.

Closing Prayer

O God, you have given us a model of family spirituality in Mary, the mother of Jesus. While on earth her life was like that of anyone else, filled with labors and the cares of the home. Always, however, she remained intimately united to her Son and cooperated in a unique way in his work. Help us to do the same in the power of your Spirit. Amen.

—Based on the Decree on the Apostolate of Lay People, no. 4

Home Study Questions

Family spirituality is fine as long as everything goes well. What about families in stress or crisis? What happens to their spiritual life?

Vatican II acknowledged the troubles families sometimes face and included these difficult times in its view of family spirituality. "Family cares should not be foreign to their spirituality, nor any other temporal interest" (Decree on the Apostolate of Lay People, no. 4). After this statement, the council invoked the passage of St. Paul that was used in the last session: "Whatever you are doing, whether speaking or acting, do everything in the name of the Lord Jesus Christ, giving thanks to God the Father through him" (Col 3:17). This doesn't mean you should minimize family problems or avoid them in the name of religion or spirituality. It means you should deal with them as part of your total life with God.

Pope John Paul II took this one step further and urged family prayer as a way to weave experience into union with Christ.

> Family prayer has for its very own object *family life itself*, which in all its varying circumstances is seen as a call from God and lived as a filial response to his call. Joys and sorrows, hopes and disappointments, births and birthday celebrations, wedding anniversaries of the parents, departures, separations and homecomings, important and far-reaching decisions, the death of those who are dear, etc.—

> all of these mark God's loving intervention in the family's history. They should be seen as suitable moments for thanksgiving, for petition, for trusting abandonment of the family into the hands of their common Father in heaven (The Christian Family in the Modern World, no. 59).

Families are so scattered today. Doesn't that make family spirituality harder to achieve?

Vatican II ordinarily spoke in terms of the so-called nuclear family, but it did not envision family as a self-contained unit, closed in on itself. The council saw the family as a center of activity reaching beyond its immediate members to society. If family members are never together, this obviously causes problems, but Vatican II put the focus on what could actually happen when the family was together rather than on the family being together all the time.

For example:

> The mission of being the primary vital cell of society has been given to the family by God himself. This mission will be accomplished if the family, by the mutual affection of its members and by family prayer, presents itself as a domestic sanctuary of the Church; if the whole family takes its part in the Church's liturgical worship; if, finally, it offers active hospitality, and practices justice and other good works for the benefit of all its brothers suffering from want (Decree on the Apostolate of Lay People, no. 11).

Carrying this further, the council frequently depicted the family as a school that benefits society.

> The family is the principal school of the social virtues which are necessary to every society (Declaration on Christian Education, no. 3).
>
> The whole family and its community life should become a kind of apprenticeship to the apostolate (Decree on the Apostolate of Lay People, no. 30).
>
> By living a true Christian life families should become seminaries for lay apostles and indeed of priestly and religious vocations (Decree on the Church's Missionary Activity, no. 19).
>
> The family is, in a sense, a school for human enrichment (Pastoral Constitution on the Church in the Modern World, no. 52).

Pope John Paul II repeated this view, stressing sacramental spirituality and its connection with family:

> The Christian family, as the "domestic church," also makes up a natural and fundamental school for formation in the faith: father and mother receive from the Sacrament of Matrimony the grace and the ministry of the Christian education of their children, before whom they bear witness and to whom they transmit both human

> and religious values. While learning their first words, children learn also the praise of God, whom they feel is near them as a loving and providential Father; while learning the first acts of love, children also learn to open themselves to others, and through the gift of self receive the sense of living as a human being. The daily life itself of a truly Christian family makes up the first "experience of Church," intended to find confirmation and development in an active and responsible process of the children's introduction into the wider ecclesial community and civil society (Exhortation on the Christian Lay Faithful, no. 62).

There is a lot of talk about extended families. How extensive was the council's view of family and family spirituality?

Vatican II didn't use the term "extended family," but it extended the term "family" to various groups who gather in faith and the spirit of Christ. Within the Catholic Church, the term is most often extended to religious communities.

> A [religious] community gathered together as a true family in the Lord's name enjoys his presence, through the love of God which is poured into their hearts by the Holy Spirit (Decree on the Up-to-Date Renewal of Religious Life, no. 15).

The council extended the spiritual character and rights of family to all families, not just Catholic or Christian families.

> Every family, in that it is a society with its own basic rights, has the right freely to organize its own religious life in the home under the control of the parents. These have the right to decide in accordance with their own religious beliefs the form of religious upbringing which is to be given to their children (Declaration on Religious Liberty, no. 5).

From a spiritual point of view, the most extended family discussed by Vatican II was the communion of saints, that family of believers consisting of those who have died and those who still live on earth.

> Being more closely united to Christ, those who dwell in heaven fix the whole Church more firmly in holiness, add to the nobility of the worship that the Church offers to God here on earth, and in many ways help in a broader building up of the Church (Constitution on the Church, no. 49).

The building up of the Church was elaborated by the council when it said that "our community with the saints joins us to Christ, from whom as from its fountain and head issues all grace and the life of the People of God itself" (no. 50).

SESSION FOUR

Biblical Spirituality: Catholic or Protestant?

Goals

- To examine common misunderstandings about Catholics and the Bible
- To review what Vatican II said about Catholics and the Bible
- To consider how Vatican II's teaching aids the spiritual life
- To put this learning into practice through action

Scripture

The Gospel of John begins with a meditation on the Word of God, who became incarnate in Jesus. This same Word is the heart of the Bible. As you listen to John's testimony, picture the Word coming from God through Jesus to you in the Bible.

John 1:1-3, 14, 16 **In the beginning was the Word; the Word was in God's presence, and the Word was God.** *(pause)*

He was present to God in the beginning. Through him all things came into being, and apart from him nothing came to be. *(pause)*

The Word became flesh and made his dwelling among us, and we have seen his glory: the glory of an only Son coming from the Father, filled with enduring love. *(pause)*

Of his fullness we have all had a share—love following upon love.

Prayer

O God, in the Sacred Scriptures you come lovingly to meet us and talk with us. Your Word is living and active and unites us with our brothers and sisters from the past and around the world today. Help us always to hear your Word and live it. We ask this through Christ our Lord. Amen.

—Based on the Dogmatic Constitution on Divine Revelation, no. 21

Catholics and the Bible

Before Vatican II the Bible was often a dividing issue between Catholics and other Christians. Since Vatican II there has been a better understanding between Catholics and Protestants. There has also been a growing desire by Catholics to nourish their spiritual lives through the Bible.

Based on your experience with the Bible since Vatican II, how would you respond to each of the following statements, which were typical before Vatican II?

"Catholics don't take the Bible literally as the Word of God."

it is the word of God but not taken literally

"Catholics aren't allowed to read the Bible privately."

not true now

"Catholics celebrate the sacraments rather than read the Word of God in the Bible."

not true

"Preaching is deemphasized in Catholic worship and is more doctrinal than biblical."

not true

"Catholic prayers are memorized rather than spontaneous, and Catholics prefer devotions to the saints to devotional reading of the Bible."

not any more but we still use memorized prayers + Devotions also, but fewer do

Vatican II Speaks

Vatican II went out of its way to demonstrate its reverence for the Bible. A copy of the Scriptures was always prominently displayed where the council met, and every session opened with a reading from Scripture. The council's most complete discussion of the Bible took place in the Dogmatic Constitution on Divine Revelation.

WORD OF GOD

Vatican II clearly affirmed the Catholic belief that the Bible is the Word of God. "Sacred Scripture is the speech of God as it is put down in writing under the breath of the Holy Spirit" (Dogmatic Constitution on Divine Revelation, no. 9).

The council also said that interpreting the Bible, that is, grasping its literal meaning, requires close attention to the human authors God used in writing it. "Seeing that, in sacred Scripture, God speaks through men in human fashion, it follows that the interpreter of sacred Scriptures, if he is to ascertain what God has wished to communicate to us, should carefully search out the meaning which the sacred writers really had in mind" (no. 12).

PRIVATE READING

Vatican II was eager for all Catholics to become acquainted with the Bible as a nourishment for their spiritual lives. To achieve this, the council initiated a new series of readings for Sunday and weekday Masses. "The treasures of the Bible are to be opened up more lavishly so that a richer fare may be provided for the faithful at the table of God's word" (The Constitution on the Sacred Liturgy, no. 51).

The spiritual purpose of this change was stated clearly in the Dogmatic Constitution on Divine Revelation. "It follows that all the preaching of the Church, as indeed the entire Christian religion, should be nourished and ruled by sacred Scripture. . . . such is the force and power of the Word of God that it can serve the Church as her support and vigor, and the children of the Church as strength for their faith, food for the soul, and a pure and lasting fount of spiritual life" (no. 21).

THE BIBLE AND SACRAMENTS

Vatican II constantly stressed the unbreakable union of the Bible and the sacraments. They are not in competition with each other but complement each other in nurturing the Christian's spiritual life. The council stated this very forcefully when it said, "The Church has always venerated the divine Scriptures as she venerated the Body of the Lord, in so far as she never ceases, particularly in the sacred liturgy, to partake of the bread of life and to offer it to the faithful from the one table of the Word of God and the Body of Christ" (Dogmatic Constitution on Divine Revelation, no. 21).

When stating the general norms for liturgical renewal, Vatican II had this to say about Scripture: "Sacred Scripture is of the greatest importance in the celebration of the liturgy. For it is from it that lessons are read and explained in the homily, and psalms are sung. It is from the scriptures that the prayers, collects, and hymns draw their inspiration and their force, and that actions and signs derive their meaning" (The Constitution on the Sacred Liturgy, no. 24).

PREACHING

Vatican II restored preaching to its rightful place of importance in Catholic worship and intended that it be based on the Scriptures read at the liturgy.

> By means of the homily the mysteries of the faith and the guiding principles of the Christian life are expounded from the sacred text during the course of the liturgical year. The homily, therefore, is to be highly esteemed as part of the liturgy itself (The Constitution on the Sacred Liturgy, no. 52).

The council also said that within the total ministry of the Word, "the liturgical homily should hold pride of place" (Dogmatic Constitution on Divine Revelation, no. 24).

THE BIBLE AND PRAYER

Vatican II encouraged more than hearing or reading the Bible. It acknowledged the importance of praying with the Bible and letting the Bible shape one's prayer. To promote this, the council recommended Bible services (The Constitution on the Sacred Liturgy, no. 35). It also encouraged personal prayer with the Bible for all the faithful, with this reminder:

> Let them remember that prayer should accompany the reading of sacred Scripture, so that a dialogue takes place between God and man (Dogmatic Constitution on Divine Revelation, no. 25).

Summing Up

Catholics may not have been very well acquainted with the Bible before Vatican II, but the council incorporated more Scripture readings into the liturgy and urged Catholics to read, study, and pray over the sacred texts as a means of spiritual growth.

How many ways does the Bible nourish Christian spirituality?

personal prayer

Liturgy of the Word

Homily reflects on scripture reading

How many ways does the Bible nourish my spirituality?

Action

To develop my biblical and liturgical spirituality, I can study the Scripture readings for Sunday Mass ahead of time, preferably with others.

To get the most out of the homily, I can discuss it with my family or friends after Mass.

To learn more about biblical spirituality, I can find out how other Christian Churches in my neighborhood study and use the Bible.

Before the Next Session

Carry out one of the Action suggestions.

Read the Home Study Questions for Session 5, pages 43–45; or read Chapter 6, Dogmatic Constitution on Divine Revelation.

Closing Prayer

O God, grant that by our reading and study of the sacred books, the treasure of revelation entrusted to your Church may more and more fill our hearts, and may we expect a new impulse of spiritual life from increased veneration of your Word, which stands forever. We ask this through Christ our Lord. Amen.

—Based on the Dogmatic Constitution on Divine Revelation, no. 26

Home Study Questions

Even though there have been advances in Bible study since Vatican II, isn't it still true that Protestants know, read, and pray the Bible more than Catholics?

Because of the traditional Protestant emphasis on the Bible, Protestants generally are more familiar with its contents than Catholics. Vatican II acknowledged the priority of Scripture for most Protestants when it said, ''A love and reverence— almost a cult—of Holy Scripture leads our brethren to a constant and diligent study of the sacred text'' (Decree on Ecumenism, no. 21).

The council also implied that Catholics have much to learn from Protestants and tried to describe this sharing as a friendly competition rather than a contest resulting in winners and losers. What the council said about professional theological dialogues is equally applicable to everyday exchanges between Catholics and Protestants: ''The way will be opened whereby a kind of 'fraternal rivalry' will incite all to a deeper realization and a clearer expression of the unfathomable riches of Christ'' (no. 11).

Isn't it true that Catholics aren't allowed to interpret the Bible for themselves?

Vatican II was aware of the history of controversy on this point and described it very sensitively: ''But when Christians separated from us affirm the divine authority of the sacred books, they think differently from us—different ones in different ways—about the relationship between the scriptures and the Church'' (no. 21).

The Catholic view, according to the council, is that interpretation of Scripture belongs to the Church as a whole. ''The whole body of the faithful who have an anointing that comes from the holy one (cf. 1 John 2:20, 27) cannot err in matters of belief'' (Dogmatic Constitution on the Church, no. 12).

The role of articulating the belief of the Church (technically called ''authentic interpretation'') belongs to the bishops. ''But the task of giving an authentic interpretation of the Word of God, whether in its written form or in the form of Tradition, has been entrusted to the living teaching office of the Church alone. Its authority in this matter is exercised in the name of Jesus Christ. Yet this Magisterium [the bishops as teachers] is not superior to the Word of God, but is its servant. It teaches only what has been handed on to it'' (Dogmatic Constitution on Divine Revelation, no. 10).

The council's position is summed up best in this statement: ''By this appreciation of the faith, aroused and sustained by the Spirit of truth, the People of God, guided by the sacred teaching authority *(magisterium)* and obeying it, receives not the mere word of men, but truly the word of God (cf. 1 Thess 2:13), the faith once for all delivered to the saints (cf. Jude 3). The People unfailingly adheres to this faith, penetrates it more deeply with right judgment, and applies it more fully in daily life'' (Dogmatic Constitution on the Church, no 12).

Why are there so many readings at Mass? Why isn't there more time to reflect on them?

The desire of Vatican II in revising the Liturgy of the Word at Mass was to expose people to more selections from the Bible. But merely reading and hearing more Scripture passages was not the primary goal. Pope Paul VI made this clear in his introduction to the Roman Missal.

> All these various ordinances are intended to stimulate ever more intensely among the faithful that hunger for the word of God which, under the guidance of the Holy Spirit, is urging the people of the New Testament towards the goal of perfect unity within the Church.

> We cherish the firm hope that, through the influence of these new arrangements, both priests and people will together prepare themselves more effectively for the celebrations of the Lord's Supper and, at the same time, will daily receive increasing nourishment from the word of God through more intensive reflection on holy Scripture. Thus, in accordance with the exhortation of the Second Vatican Council, the sacred writings will be recognized by all as the unfailing source of the spiritual life.

The importance of silence was acknowledged in the introduction to the second edition of the Lectionary, the book of readings used at Mass.

> The liturgy of the word should be celebrated in a way that favors meditation. Any kind of haste is to be totally avoided, for it impedes recollection. Dialogue between God and his people, with the help of the Holy Spirit, requires short periods of silence, adjusted to the assembly, during which the heart opens to the word of God and prayerful response takes shape (no. 28).

If the homily is so important, why aren't homilies better?

Vatican II stressed the importance of the homily but left it to the Church after the council to improve the quality of preaching. The bishops in the United States, through their Priestly Life and Ministry Committee, have offered guidelines for preaching that discuss the assembly, the homily, and the preacher. Regarding homily preparation, they recommend Homily Preparation Groups composed of parishioners who help the homilist prepare the homily by offering their own insights into the Scripture readings, suggesting examples and applications, and offering an evaluation of the content and delivery of the homily. The guildelines also list six ''nonnegotiables'' for good preaching preparation: time, prayer, study, organization, concreteness, and evaluation (Fulfilled in Your Hearing, pp. 36–39).

The bishops also acknowledged how awesome a task it is to proclaim God's Word effectively.

> We too stand in sacred space, aware of our personal inadequacy, yet willing to share how the scriptural story has become integrated into our thoughts and actions while we walked among those who turn their faces toward us. The words we speak are human words describing how God's action has become apparent to us this week. Is it any wonder then that excitement and tension fill us in the moments before we preach? With a final deep breath may we also breathe in the Spirit of God who will animate our human words with divine power (p. 43).

Liturgical Spirituality: Spectators or Participants?

Goals

- To review the principles of Vatican II's liturgical renewal
- To learn the primary spiritual concerns of Vatican II's liturgical renewal
- To put this learning into practice through action

Scripture

When the first Christians reflected on their experience of worship, they came to some profound insights. Many of these were put together in the Letter to the Hebrews. For example, listen to this passage:

Hebrews 12:18-20, 22-24 **You have not drawn near to an untouchable mountain and blazing fire, nor gloomy darkness and storm and trumpet blast, nor a voice speaking words such that those who heard begged that they be not addressed to them, for they could not bear to hear the command.**

No, you have drawn near to Mount Zion and the city of the living God, the heavenly Jerusalem, to myriads of angels in festal gathering, to the assembly of the first-born enrolled in heaven, to God the judge of all, to the spirits of the just made perfect, to Jesus, mediator of a new covenant.

Prayer

O God, our earthly liturgies are a foretaste of that heavenly liturgy to which we journey as pilgrims. With all the holy ones we sing a hymn of glory to the Lord, venerate the memory of the saints who have gone before us, and share in the communion of life without end, offered to us through Christ our Lord. Amen.

—Based on The Constitution on the Sacred Liturgy, no. 8

Our Experience of Liturgy

The liturgical changes of Vatican II were intended to deepen the spiritual lives of Catholics. The principles listed below were set forth by Vatican II to guide the liturgical renewal. Drawing on your experience of the liturgy, rank these principles in the order that you feel is most important for liturgical spirituality.

____Liturgical services are not private functions but are celebrations of the Church (The Constitution on the Sacred Liturgy, no. 26).

____All the faithful should be led to that full, conscious, and active participation in liturgical celebrations which is demanded by the very nature of the liturgy (no. 14).

____Provided that the substantial unity of the Roman Rite is preserved, provisions shall be made . . . for legitimate variations and adaptations to different groups, regions, and peoples (no. 38).

____When the liturgy is celebrated, something more is required than the laws governing valid and lawful celebration (no. 11).

____Devotions should be so drawn up that they harmonize with the liturgical seasons, accord with the sacred liturgy, are in some way derived from it, and lead the people to it (no. 13).

____In order that the liturgy may be able to produce its full effects, it is necessary that the faithful come to it with proper dispositions, that their minds be attuned to their voices, and that they cooperate with heavenly grace lest they receive it in vain (no. 11).

____Pastors should see to it that the principal hours of the Divine Office, especially Vespers, are celebrated in common in church on Sundays and the more solemn feasts (no. 100).

____During Lent, penance should be not only internal and individual but also external and social. The practice of penance should be suited to the present day, to different regions, and to individual circumstances (no. 110).

____Liturgical music, as a combination of sacred music and words, forms a necessary or integral part of the liturgy (no. 112).

____The art of our own times from every race and country shall be given free scope in the Church (no. 123).

Our group consensus is:

1.____________________

2.____________________

3.____________________

Vatican II Speaks

People knew something was happening at Vatican II when changes in the liturgy began to occur even before the council ended. Many people found that these changes were not adequately explained. In particular the spiritual motive behind the liturgical changes was often overlooked in favor of "doing things right." Vatican II expressed the spiritual purpose of the liturgy this way:

> The liturgy daily builds up those who are in the Church, making of them a holy temple of the Lord, a dwelling-place for God in the Spirit, to the mature measure of the fullness of Christ (The Constitution on the Sacred Liturgy, no. 2).

KEY PRINCIPLE

In order to do this, the liturgical changes of Vatican II were guided by several principles. The one stated most frequently and with greatest emphasis was this:

> In the restoration and promotion of the sacred liturgy the full and active participation by all the people is the aim to be considered before all else, for it is the primary and indispensable source from which the faithful are to derive the true Christian spirit (no. 14).

KEY STRATEGY

To accomplish this goal, ''the rites . . . should be short, clear, and free from useless repetitions. They should be within the people's comprehension and normally should not require much explanation'' (no. 34).

KEY CONNECTION

The council extolled the liturgy but did not isolate it from the rest of people's lives. In its most famous statement on the liturgy, Vatican II stressed the intimate connection between liturgy and the rest of the Church's life. ''The liturgy is the summit toward which the activity of the Church is directed; it is also the fount from which all her power flows'' (no. 10).

Summing Up

Vatican II saw the liturgy as the core of the Church's spiritual renewal. The new emphasis that Vatican II provided was on the full, conscious, and active participation of the faithful.

What liturgical principles have I learned from this discussion that will aid my spirituality?

____

____

____

How does my spirituality come to expression in the liturgy?

____

____

____

Action

To take a more active role in the liturgy, I can volunteer for one of the liturgical ministries or do my part as a participant more fully.

To give more of a liturgical spirit to my life, I can participate in a parish liturgy on the next civil holiday or major Church feast.

To broaden my experience of the liturgy, I can participate in a sacramental celebration of baptism, anointing, reconciliation, or the Rite of Christian Initiation of Adults.

Before the Next Session

Carry out one of the Action suggestions.

Complete the following statements.

For me, the most important learning of the last five sessions is

____

____

____

____

One activity the group could perform to put this into practice is

____

____

____

____

Closing Prayer

O God, you invite us to the liturgy not as strangers or silent spectators but as full participants. Move us to do our part to make each liturgy truly a foretaste of that eternal liturgy for which we prepare. We ask this through Christ our Lord. Amen.

—Based on The Constitution on the Sacred Liturgy, no. 47

Home Study Questions

What exactly is the liturgy? What is included in it?

Liturgy refers to the official and public worship of the Church. "Therefore, liturgical services pertain to the whole Body of the Church. They manifest it, and have effects upon it" (The Constitution on the Sacred Liturgy, no. 25).

In the Catholic tradition the liturgy consists of the seven sacraments and the Liturgy of the Hours (Divine Office). The Eucharist is the central sacrament and along with baptism and confirmation constitute the sacraments of initiation. Penance, anointing, marriage, and ordination are the other sacraments. The Liturgy of the Hours is explained in the Home Study section of Session 4.

Those things that are used in celebrating the liturgy are often given a special designation. Thus water, oil, bread, wine, candles, blessings, and vestments are called sacramentals; the music, art, architecture, and ritual books of worship are called sacred; the schedule of feasts and celebrations (Advent, Lent, Easter, Pentecost) comprises the liturgical year.

Where do devotions fit in?

Vatican II acknowledged that "the spiritual life is not limited solely to participation in the liturgy" (no. 12).

Devotions have played a big part in the spiritual life of many Catholics. Vatican II "highly recommended" popular devotions so long as such devotions "harmonize with the liturgical seasons, accord with the sacred liturgy, are in some way derived from it, and lead the people to it, since in fact the liturgy by its very nature is far superior to any of them" (no. 13).

Devotion to saints holds a special place because "to look on the life of those who have faithfully followed Christ is to be inspired with a new reason for seeking the city which is to come (cf. Heb 13:14 and 11:10), while at the same time we are taught to know a most safe path by which, despite the vicissitudes of the world, and in keeping with the state of life and condition proper to each of us, we will be able to arrive at perfect union with Christ, that is, holiness" (Dogmatic Constitution on the Church, no. 50).

Of course, devotion to Mary, the mother of Jesus, is paramount among honor shown to the saints. Vatican II urged that "the cult, especially the liturgical cult, of the Blessed Virgin, be generously fostered, and that the practices and exercises of devotion towards her, recommended by the teaching authority of the Church in the course of centuries be highly esteemed, and that those decrees, which were given in the early days regarding the cult images of Christ, the Blessed Virgin, and the saints, be religiously observed" (no. 67).

At the same time, the council recalled that "true devotion consists neither in sterile or transitory affection, nor in a certain vain credulity, but proceeds from true faith, by which we are led to recognize the excellence of the Mother of God, and we are moved to a filial love towards our mother and to the imitation of her virtues" (no. 67).

In this ecumenical age how can liturgical spirituality be shared with Protestants?

Vatican II's general position was:

> Catholics must gladly acknowledge and esteem the truly Christian endowments from our common heritage which are to be found among our separated brethren. It is right and salutary to recognize the riches of Christ and virtuous works in the lives of others who are bearing witness to Christ, sometimes even to the shedding of their blood. For God is always wonderful in his works and worthy of praise. Nor should we forget that anything wrought by the grace of the Holy Spirit in the hearts of our separated brethren can contribute to our own edification. Whatever is truly Christian is never contrary to what genuinely belongs to the faith; indeed, it can always bring a more perfect realization of the very mystery of Christ and the Church (Decree on Ecumenism, no. 4).

Turning to Catholics, the council stated:

> The faithful should remember that they promote union among Christians better, that indeed they live it better, when they try to live holier lives according to the Gospel (no. 7).

Applying this principle, the council affirmed the "recognized custom for Catholics to meet for frequent recourse to that prayer for unity of the Church." It also acknowledged that "in certain circumstances, such as in prayer services 'for unity' and during ecumenical gatherings, it is allowable, indeed desirable that Catholics should join in prayer with their separated brethren" (no. 8).

Sacramental sharing, however, poses a different problem: "Worship in common is not to be considered as a means to be used indiscriminately for the restoration of unity among Christians." The council articulated two principles in this area.

> There are two main principles upon which the practice of such common worship depends: first, that of the unity of the Church which ought to be expressed; the second, that of the sharing in the means of grace. The expression of unity very generally forbids common worship. Grace to be obtained sometimes commends it (no. 8).

Knowing which is which is left to the bishops to decide.

The growth of "spiritual ecumenism" in the years after the council prompted a further clarification from the Vatican Secretariat for Christian Unity. Concerning the possibility of admitting other Christians to the Eucharist in a Catholic liturgy, the Secretariat first stressed the "strict relationship between the mystery of the Church and the mystery of the Eucharist." Then it acknowledged that this principle would not be violated if the Christians admitted to Communion

1. have a faith in the sacrament in conformity with that of the Church,
2. experience a serious spiritual need for Eucharistic sustenance,
3. for a prolonged time are unable to have recourse to a minister of their own community,
4. ask for the sacrament of their own accord.

Apart from Mass, what has been the most important change in liturgical spirituality since Vatican II?

For many Catholics it has been the Rite of Christian Initiation of Adults (RCIA). Vatican II merely called for its restoration: "The catechumenate for adults, comprising several distinct steps, is to be restored and brought into use at the direction of the local ordinary [bishop]" (The Constitution on the Sacred Liturgy, no. 64).

When the Rite was finally completed and began to be implemented, many found in it a total experience of spiritual growth for themselves as well as for those who sought initiation into the Catholic Church. This is not surprising, for the main principles governing the RCIA summarize the essence of Vatican II's approach to liturgical spirituality.

> The initiation of catechumens takes place step by step in the midst of the community of the faithful. Together with the catechumens, the faithful reflect upon the value of the paschal mystery, renew their own conversion, and by their example lead the catechumens to obey the Holy Spirit more generously.
>
> The rite of initiation is suited to the spiritual journey of adults, which varies according to the many forms of God's grace, the free cooperation of the individuals, the action of the Church, and the circumstances of time and place.
>
> On this journey, besides the period for making inquiry and maturing, there are stages or steps by which the catechumen moves forward, as it were, through a gateway or up another step.
>
> These stages, steps, or gateways are to be considered as major, more serious moments of initiation and are marked by liturgical rites.
>
> The final period goes through the whole Easter season and is called the post-baptismal catechesis or "mystagogia." It is a time for deepening the Christian experience, for gaining spiritual fruit, and for entering more closely into the life and unity of the community of the faithful (Rite of Christian Initiation of Adults, nos. 4–7).

SESSION SIX

Answering the Call to Holiness: Now What?

Goals

- To formulate the consensus of the group about what they have learned in the previous sessions
- To determine whether the group wants to carry out an action that will put their learning into practice
- To celebrate in prayer the sharing of the last five sessions

Scripture

Everyone who hears the word of God is expected to put it into practice.

James 1:22-25 **Be doers of the word and not hearers only, deluding yourselves. For if anyone is a hearer of the word and not a doer, he is like a man who looks at his own face in a mirror. He sees himself, then goes off and promptly forgets what he looked like. But the one who peers into the perfect law of freedom and perseveres, and is not a hearer who forgets but a doer who acts, such a one shall be blessed in what he does.**

Prayer

O God, who spoke and the world was created, who promised and the covenant was fashioned, who came and people were saved, do not let us become forgetful listeners, but help us to put your word into practice, now and all the days of our life. Amen.

Learning into Action

1. Go back to page 42 and read your statements about your own learning and a possible group action.
2. Write those statements with any changes you now wish to make on the following lines:

Statement of Learning	***Proposed Action***
______________________	______________________
______________________	______________________
______________________	______________________
______________________	______________________

3. Designate one person to write each person's responses (from the lines above) on a sheet of tablet paper.

4. When everyone's responses have been recorded, study them for a few moments.

5. Has more than one person mentioned the same learning or the same action? If so, the designated person puts one check beside this response for each person who mentioned it.

6. If the response with the most checks is agreeable to everyone, allowing for minor additions or changes, this is the consensus of the group.

7. If there is no common response or if none is agreeable to the group, is there a way to combine some of the responses? Take your time in doing this.

8. If a combined statement is suggested, the designated person writes it on the tablet. Is it agreeable to everyone, allowing for minor changes or additions? If so, this is the consensus of the group.

9. If no consensus on anything is possible, then this is the result of the group's deliberation.

10. Designate one person from each subgroup to report the consensus to the large group.

SUBGROUP DISCUSSIONS

Notes/comments from this discussion, including the subgroup's consensus Statement of Learning and Proposed Action.

____

____

____

____

____

____

____

LARGE GROUP DISCUSSION

Statement of Learning — *Proposed Action*

(Group 1 Consensus)

______________________ ______________________

______________________ ______________________

______________________ ______________________

(Group 2 Consensus)

______________________ ______________________

______________________ ______________________

______________________ ______________________

Notes/Comments

____

____

____

FINAL CONSENSUS

Statement of Learning — *Proposed Action*

______________________ ______________________

______________________ ______________________

______________________ ______________________

LOOKING AHEAD

A group action is highly recommended as a conclusion to this program, *Called to Holiness;* however, the decision for or against a group action is entirely up to the group.

To help the group or part of the group develop the action proposal into a working plan and carry it out, the optional session, "Learning into Action," follows.

The optional session goes beyond the convener's commitment to ***Vatican II—Act II.*** The convener may agree to continue, or a new convener must be chosen.

If a group action is to be carried out, three subgroups should be formed to decide on (1) the basis in Vatican II for the intended action, (2) what must be done to accomplish the action, and (3) what the intended outcome is to be.

Each person should read the section Preparing for Action, stay in touch with their subgroup to exchange ideas and information, and bring their written ideas to the session.

Write the final consensus Statement of Learning and Proposed Action on page 48 in your booklet.

Scripture and Closing Prayer

Tobit 13:13-16

**Go, then, rejoice over the children of the righteous,
who shall all be gathered together
and shall bless the Lord of the ages.
Happy are those who love you,
and happy those who rejoice in your prosperity.**

**Happy are all the men who shall grieve over you,
over all your chastisements,
For they shall rejoice in you
as they behold all your joy forever.**

**My spirit blesses the Lord, the great King;
Jerusalem shall be rebuilt as his home forever.
Happy for me if a remnant of my offspring survive
to see your glory and to praise the King of heaven!**

What have the last six sessions meant to me?

____

____

____

How am I different because of these sessions?

____

____

____

Colossians 3:12-16 **Because you are God's chosen ones, holy and beloved, clothe yourselves with heartfelt mercy, with kindness, humility, meekness; forgive whatever grievances you have against one another. Forgive as the Lord has forgiven you. Over all these virtues put on love, which binds the rest together and makes them**

perfect. Christ's peace must reign in your hearts, since as members of one body you have been called to that peace. Dedicate yourselves to thankfulness. Let the word of Christ, rich as it is, dwell in you. In wisdom made perfect, instruct and admonish one another. Sing gratefully to God from your hearts in psalms, hymns, and inspired songs.

Exchange a greeting of peace.

SESSION SEVEN

Learning into Action: An Optional Exercise

Preparing for Action

Read this Preparing for Action section, talk to other members of your subgroup, and bring your written ideas to the session.

A meaningful and satisfying group action should be well planned. In the ***Vatican II—Act II*** program the essential ingredients for a well-planned action are the following:

Statement of learning. This is the Final Consensus statement from page 48.

For example, the group's consensus statement might be that "A person's daily activities should be a source of holiness and spiritual growth."

Proposed action. This is the Proposed Action statement from page 48.

For example, "Our group will continue to meet to help each other reflect on our daily activities so we can grow spiritually through them."

Basis in Vatican II. This includes the chapters in specific documents where the basis for the Statement of Learning and Proposed Action can be found.

Plan of action. This is a list of steps needed to accomplish the action.

For example, the group would have to decide

1. when and where to meet;
2. how long each meeting will last;
3. how to spend the time, e.g., each meeting devoted to just one person, each person share something at each meeting, the group divide into smaller units for more discussion;
4. whether to include time for prayer during the meeting;
5. how each member will inform the group of action taken on their suggestions;
6. when to terminate the group's action.

Intended outcome. This identifies the specific outcome the group plans to accomplish. The group should make sure that the goal is realistic.

For example, the group will meet once a week for one month and then evaluate its experience.

Prayer

Begin the session with this Prayer.

O God of patience and hope, you urge us to think creatively, to act courageously, and to trust confidently. When we make the smallest effort, you bless it generously; and when we are unable to act together, you give us more time. Stay with us as we spread the benefits of what we have learned to others. We ask this through Christ our Lord. Amen.

Developing the Action

(20 minutes) Write in the final consensus Statement of Learning and Proposed Action from Session 6, page 48.

Statement of Learning	***Proposed Action***
______________________	______________________
______________________	______________________
______________________	______________________
______________________	______________________

The subgroups should meet for a few minutes to finalize their statements.

Basis in Vatican II

Ask subgroup 1 to describe the Basis in Vatican II which they developed. All should record their findings on the lines below.

____

____

____

Plan of Action

Ask subgroup 2 to describe their Plan of Action. All should record the subgroup's plan.

Specific steps:________________________________

____

____

____

Resources needed:____

____

____

____

People responsible:_______________________________________

____

____

____

Time frame:____

____

____

____

Intended Outcome

Ask subgroup 3 to report their Intended Outcome. Record the Intended Outcome below.

____

____

____

____

SUBGROUP DISCUSSIONS

(20 minutes) The subgroups should now separate. Each subgroup will discuss among themselves the findings or proposals of another subgroup.

The convener will spend time with each subgroup, answer questions, and keep the subgroups aware of the time.

Basis in Vatican II

Do the passages selected establish the basis for the action agreed to?

____

____

Are there other passages you would recommend?____________________

____

____

Plan of Action

Can the specific actions be carried out?________________________

____

____

Will they achieve the goal?___________________________________

____

____

Would you suggest others?____________________________________

____

____

Are the necessary resources available?_________________________

____

____

Are other resources needed?__________________________________

____

____

Is it clear who is responsible for each step?_____________________

____

____

Is the time frame realistic?__________________________________

____

____

Intended Outcome

Is the intended outcome clear?________________________________

____

____

Are the standards for judging success easily recognizable?__________

____

____

Is the time for completing the project realistic?________________

____

____

(10 minutes) Break

When the large group has reconvened, ask each subgroup to add their insights to the original findings and proposals. Members of the large group may want to comment, either on the original findings and proposals or on the new insights gained from the subgroup discussions.

REFINING THE PLAN

(20 minutes) Each subgroup should now meet to discuss the new ideas gained and to refine their part of the proposed action. This will be the Final Plan.

At the end of this time, the subgroups should present the Final Plan to the entire group, and everyone should record it on the lines below.

Final Plan

Basis in Vatican II

____

____

____

____

Plan of Action

____

____

____

____

Intended Outcome

____

____

____

____

If any member, following his or her own best judgment in the light of Vatican II, has reservations about any part of the plan, these should be discussed now. The particular member may choose to work with the group despite the reservations or may choose to do something else.

Likewise, if the group has been unable to agree about the plan as a whole, this should not be judged a failure. It is simply a fact. The learning and the sharing of different viewpoints and values should be affirmed and celebrated.

Closing Prayer

After a moment of silence to feel God's presence, recite this Closing Prayer together.

O gracious God, we give you thanks that we have spent this time together. May we use every opportunity you give us to spread your word and nourish your life in others as we work for the coming of your kingdom, through Christ our Lord. Amen.

Reviewing the Action

If the action is to be carried out, group members will be in close contact with one another during that period of time. When the action has been completed, it is recommended that the group come together one last time to learn from each other about the experience and to celebrate this action carried out in the spirit of Vatican II.

The following questions may help guide your reflection.

Overall, how do I feel about our group's action?

____

____

____

____

____

How do I feel about my part in it?

____

____

____

____

____

What could we have done differently that would have made it more successful?

____

____

____

____

____

What was the best thing that happened as a result of the project?

____

____

____

____

____

What did I learn from this project about myself?

____

____

____

____

____

about Vatican II?

____

____

____

____

____

***about the topic* Called to Holiness?**

____

____

____

____

____

Summary

God calls each person to a life of holiness.

Persons respond to God's call in the particular circumstances of their lives and use these occasions to grow in holiness.

Christian spirituality is centered on Jesus and involves a share in his threefold work as a Priest, Prophet, and Pastor.

Family spirituality embraces all the relationships that make up a family, including those between spouses, between parents and children, among children, with extended family, special friends, and those who are divorced, separated, or widowed.

The Bible nourishes spirituality primarily through its stories and its use in the liturgy.

Liturgical spirituality requires that people participate in the liturgy rather than passively receive its benefits.

The Vatican II Documents

The Constitution on the Sacred Liturgy ***(Sacrosanctum Concilium)***

Two guiding principles govern the restoration of rites for sacraments and Liturgy of the Hours: revisions should lead to the full, conscious, and active participation of the faithful and rites should be simple and intelligible.

Dogmatic Constitution on the Church ***(Lumen Gentium)***

The Church is a sign of the mystery of God's life in the world; the Church consists of all the baptized; all are called to holiness and have a role to play in the mission of the Church, although in different ways; Mary is the model and mother of the Church.

Dogmatic Constitution on Divine Revelation ***(Dei Verbum)***

There is one revelation of God which comes through the twin sources of Scripture and Tradition; Scripture should be central in the daily life of the faithful, venerated equally with the Eucharist.

Pastoral Constitution on the Church in the Modern World ***(Gaudium et Spes)***

The Church has a distinctive contribution to make to human dignity, human community, and human activity by interpreting the signs of the times in light of the gospel; the Church gives to and receives from society in seeking solutions to urgent problems.

Decree on the Means of Social Communication ***(Inter Mirifica)***

Modern communications media are valuable aids in linking people together and spreading the gospel.

Decree on the Catholic Eastern Churches ***(Orientalium Ecclesiarum)***

The Churches of the East are respected for their distinctive rites, theological emphases, and spiritual contributions; Catholics of the West may share their sacraments.

Decree on Ecumenism *(Unitatis Redintegratio)*

Catholic participation in ecumenism is guided by the belief that the fullness of Christ's Church subsists in the Roman Catholic Church; Protestant Churches and communities are a means of grace and salvation; Catholics are partly responsible for divisions with Protestants; every effort at every level should be made to achieve unity, although sharing the Eucharist is not yet possible; Catholics should develop an ecumenical spirit without compromising or misrepresenting the truth.

Decree on the Pastoral Office of Bishops in the Church *(Christus Dominus)*

Bishops have collegial bonds with one another and the Pope; the bishop's primary duty is to proclaim God's word; bishops have responsibility to the universal Church, the national Church, and their own diocese.

Decree on the Training of Priests *(Optatam Totius)*

Priestly training should be pastoral; the whole Church is involved in vocation recruitment and support.

Decree on the Up-to-Date Renewal of Religious Life *(Perfectae Caritatis)*

Religious orders should revise their constitutions by returning to the charism of their founder, taking account of modern conditions, and involving all their members.

Decree on the Apostolate of Lay People *(Apostolicam Actuositatem)*

The laity's distinct role is in society although they have the right and duty to use their gifts in the Church also; there are many forms and areas of the lay apostolate; spiritual formation and preparation for lay activity are essential.

Decree on the Church's Missionary Activity *(Ad Gentes Divinitus)*

The Church is missionary by nature; the primary forms of its mission activity are witness, preaching and worship, community; the whole Church should cooperate in carrying out missionary activity.

Decree on the Ministry and Life of Priests *(Presbyterorum Ordinis)*

The priest is a representative of the bishop and shares collegial bonds with other priests; the priest's primary role is to preach the word and celebrate the sacraments; the ministry is the main source of a priest's spirituality.

Declaration on Christian Education *(Gravissimum Educationis)*

Every person has a right to education; parents have a right to determine the education of their children; governments and Churches should help parents exercise their rights.

Declaration on the Relation of the Church to Non-Christian Religions *(Nostra Aetate)*

God's truth and grace are found in other religions; this is the basis for cooperation and dialogue; Jews have a special relationship with Christians and should not be held responsible for the death of Jesus.

Declaration on Religious Liberty *(Dignitatis Humanae)*

Modern awareness of human dignity and freedom of conscience coincide with God's revelation; no one should be prevented from worshiping according to conscience or be forced to worship against conscience.

The complete documents of Vatican II are available in *Vatican Council II: The Conciliar and Post Conciliar Documents,* 1988 rev. ed., Austin Flannery, ed. (Northport, N.Y.: Costello, 1987).

Other documents referred to in this book and written after the council are available in *Vatican Council II: More Post Conciliar Documents,* Austin Flannery, ed. (Northport, N.Y.: Costello, 1982).

Individual documents may be purchased from the United States Catholic Conference, 3211 Fourth St. N.E., Washington, DC 20017-1194.

Notes